Cornelius T. Mouse and Sons

Written by Christopher A. Lane
Illustrated by Sharon Dahl

A SonFlower Book

VICTOR BOOKS®
A DIVISION OF SCRIPTURE PRESS PUBLICATIONS INC.
USA CANADA ENGLAND

Dedicated
to my parents, Carl and Ann.
For passing down the blessing.

WS CCC

KIDDERMINSTER KINGDOM TALES
King Leonard's Celebration
Sir Humphrey's Honeystands
Nicholas and His Neighbors
Cornelius T. Mouse & Sons

1 2 3 4 5 6 7 8 9 10   Printing/Year   94   93   92   91   90

ISBN: 0-89693-844-1
90-189103

VICTOR BOOKS
A division of SP Publications, Inc.
Wheaton, Illinois 60187

Cornelius T. Mouse and Sons

There was once a mouse named Cornelius who lived with his two sons, Samuel and Timothy, on a sprawling estate in the countryside in the Kingdom of Kidderminster. Cornelius was a very prosperous mouse who owned a thriving apple orchard. Spread out across his land were rows and rows of tall trees loaded with bright, round apples. Dark-red, pale-pink, brilliant-green, and sparkling-gold fruit covered the rolling hills.

Cornelius also operated a cheeseworks, where cheese was made. It was a long wooden building located in a clearing between the Mouseintosh and Granny Mouse apple trees. Under his careful supervision, workers carefully combined the curds of soured milk with tasty seasonings, pressed them together into rounds, and stored the soon-to-be cheese in the damp, dark cellar below.

Cornelius and his sons lived in a large home which sat atop a grass-covered hill overlooking the estate. It had many bedrooms, a den, a study where Cornelius attended to his apple and cheese business, and two kitchens—one for fixing snacks and the other for preparing meals.

There was also a library, and that was Cornelius' favorite room of all. It was filled from one end to the other with books and had a wide window which looked out across his orchard. Many an evening would find Cornelius seated in a tall over-stuffed armchair, reading away the hours.

While Cornelius was quite proud of his estate, his orchard, and his cheeseworks, he was most proud of his sons, Samuel and Timothy. Cornelius loved and prized them above all else. "Without them," he often said, "my life would be like apple cider without any apples, or a cheese sandwich made only with dry slices of bread and no cheese."

Samuel, his elder son, was a serious sort who had taken a keen interest in cheese-making when he was very young. On most any day he could be found in the cheeseworks, experimenting with special ingredients and developing new flavors.

His younger brother, Timothy, on the other hand, had absolutely no interest in cheesemaking—or work of any kind, for that matter. He said, "This estate is dull— life in the country is for old gophers." However, despite his lack of interest, Timothy had a real eye for apples, and worked in the orchard for his father.

One cool, crisp fall afternoon, Cornelius finished his work early. "Ah," the mouse said to himself with a smile, "my business is running smoothly. The apples are plump and ripe for the picking, and the cheese looks to be coming along nicely."

Closing the record books and sheathing his fountain pen, Cornelius reached for his pocket watch.

"And it's only just now teatime." A broad smile crossed the mouse's face and a boyish glimmer filled his eyes. "It's off to the library," he said gayly, rising from his seat. "Books await, I mustn't be late."

After locking his money box and closing the door to the study, Cornelius stopped by the treats kitchen to prepare a snack, and then proceeded to the library. With a mug of hot apple cider in one hand and a steaming cheese scone in the other, he browsed the shelves of the library.

"Let me see," he said, sipping his cider. "What shall it be today? *The Rise and Fall of the Rodent Empire?* Mmm, too dry. A poem by Shortfellow? Perhaps tomorrow. Say, how about a story, that's the ticket! *The Porcupine's Progress . . . Of Mice and Mallards . . .* Ah, here we go—*King Leonard's Celebration.*"

Cornelius settled into his comfortable armchair and with a contented sigh opened the book and began to read.

"*There was a lion king who ruled over all the beasts of the Kingdom of Kidderminster. His name was Leonard, and he lived in a majestic castle high atop a mountain in the center of a jungle.*"

Suddenly there was a tap at the door.

"Mr. Cornelius," a voice called out. He recognized it as his maid, Mrs. Wiggins, a kindly kangaroo rat.

"Come in, Mrs. Wiggins," he replied.

The door opened. "Sir," Mrs. Wiggins said politely, "the Beaver Brothers are here with your sign."

"Oh, very good," Cornelius said excitedly. "Let's have a look, shall we?"

The beavers carried it in. The sign, which had been skillfully carved out of a solid piece of oak, was engraved with tall, stylish letters. It read—"Cornelius T. Mouse & Sons: Apples by the Bushel and Cheese by the Wheel."

"My, but it's handsome," Cornelius said, shaking his head. "And won't the boys be surprised?"

That evening after supper, Cornelius rose from his seat and brought a mysterious-looking, cloth-covered stand into the dining room.

"My sons, I am pleased to announce the formation of a new company," he said, pulling the cloth from the sign.

"Cornelius T. Mouse & Sons," the two young mice read in unison, *"Apples by the Bushel and Cheese by the Wheel."*

"Samuel, henceforth, you shall be my head cheesemaker," he stated proudly, "and, Timothy, you shall be my chief appler. And these," he said, pulling two gold rings from his pocket, "shall be the sign of our new partnership." And he placed the rings on their fingers.

"Thank you, Father," Samuel said with wide eyes. "I won't let you down."

"I am confident that you won't," Cornelius said. He smiled and turned to his other son.

"And, Timothy—"

Then he stopped. Timothy was looking out the tall windows.

"Is something bothering you, Timothy?" Cornelius asked.

" . . . I've been thinking for a long time, Father. I didn't know you were going to make us partners this—this soon."

Cornelius was puzzled. "But, Son, I thought you wanted—"

"I *don't* want to be your partner," Timothy said.

"What?"

"Now that I've grown up, I want to move away to the city," he explained.

Cornelius blinked several times, and his legs began to wobble. He felt like he was going to fall down. He sat down in a nearby chair.

"Perhaps you could give me my share of the business in coins, father. That would put me well on my way."

Cornelius stared at Timothy for a long moment. "I love you, Son." Then they silently walked upstairs to the study. After fiddling with the key, Cornelius opened his money box and counted out a tall stack of gold coins.

"Be careful with these coins," Cornelius warned. "They are your inheritance. Not something to be spent foolishly."

The young mouse nodded and left the study. Sinking into his chair, Cornelius put his face into his hands. "So much for Cornelius T. Mouse & Sons," he muttered.

Timothy left early the next morning on the stagecoach headed for Varmintsville, a large city far away. Many days and nights the coach traveled.

Finally, the stagecoach reached its destination, and a uniformed porcupine scrambled to open the door.

"All out for Varmintsville!" he shouted.

Timothy woke with a start and snatched up his blue suitcase. Stepping off the stagecoach, he took his first look at the big city. It had rows and rows of tall buildings that reminded Timothy of castles. The streets were busy with carriages and horses, and animals of all shapes and sizes moved briskly down the crowded walks.

"What a wonderful place to live," Timothy thought. "Not anything like our dull home in the country. It's simply brimming with excitement."

Timothy wasted no time establishing himself in his new home. He took a room at the Ritzy Rodent, the most expensive hotel in town, and immediately went on a shopping expedition to Mousey's Department Store. He purchased all sorts of fine clothes, jewelry, and nifty gadgets. He had his whiskers trimmed, his ears pressed, his tail straightened, and ordered a moussage. He even went so far as to buy a spiffy red carriage which he used to zip about town. Everywhere he went, he bought whatever pleased his eye, grabbing handfuls of coins from his wallet to pay for it all.

Every evening, Timothy threw an extravagant party so that he could make new friends in the city. He ordered cartloads of snacks, exotic fruits and drinks, cakes and pastries, and hired a band of rats to provide musical entertainment. When the animals of Varmintsville learned of Timothy's wealth and generosity, they flocked to his parties. Soon Timothy became the talk of the town.

Back at the estate, Cornelius was very concerned about Timothy. With each passing day, he found it harder to keep his mind on his work. During the daylight, he would often walk out to the main road and look to see if his son were returning. Many an evening he would skip his supper and head straight to bed. But try as he might, he could not get to sleep. He would lie on his back, turning to one side and then the other. He thought sleepy thoughts, and even counted apples and cheese wheels. Nothing seemed to help.

"This is ridiculous," he would snort, rising from bed. "I've never had trouble sleeping before."

Putting on his slippers and robe, he would pad off down the hall to the library, knowing that if there were anything which would cure his sleeplessness, it would be a tasty snack and a nice thick book. Seated in the tall overstuffed armchair, he would munch on a slice of apple bread and try to read. But it was no use. His mind was elsewhere.

"I wonder where Timothy is," he would whisper to himself. "I do hope he is safe." Then, laying the book aside, Cornelius would sit for hours, staring out the wide window, too sad to sleep or even read.

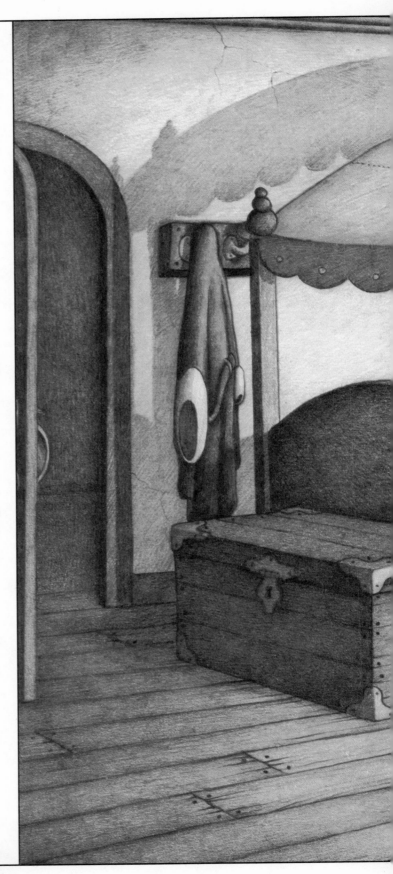

Meanwhile, Timothy became the most popular mouse in all of Varmintsville because of his wild parties.

Then, one morning as he was getting ready to go on another shopping spree, Timothy opened his wallet to get a few coins.

He gasped. It was empty! He had spent his entire inheritance in a few short months!

In order to pay his huge bills, Timothy had to return all the things he had purchased, even his spiffy red carriage. In fact, his bills were so great that he was forced to give up his gold ring, the one his father had given him. And when the manager of the Ritzy Rodent learned that the young mouse had run out of coins, he had the bellmice toss Timothy out.

He got up painfully and headed down a small street. Though he had been much too busy rushing about town, shopping and throwing parties, to notice, times had gotten tough in the city. Food and coins were now quite scarce and many rodents didn't have jobs. From the street Timothy could see down alleyways full of needy animals using newspapers for blankets and begging for money.

Suddenly one of his city friends saw him. "Timothy! What are you doing in this part of town? Anyway, I'm so glad I saw you! Listen, I—I lost my wallet. Could I borrow a bit—"

And of course Timothy couldn't help him, or any of the rest of his friends.

And when they heard that he would no longer be throwing nightly parties, they deserted him. He was poor and all alone on the streets of Varmintsville.

"What ever shall I do now?" he wondered.

That very day Cornelius had been sitting at his desk all morning trying to attend to his work. There were apples to inventory and cheese wheels to ship. Yet he could not keep his mind on business.

"Excuse me, sir," Mrs. Wiggins said, entering with a tray of refreshments. "I thought you might enjoy some tea and biscuits."

"Yes," he said, motioning for her to come in. "I can't seem to get any work done anyway."

"Are you worried about Timothy?" she asked quietly, setting the tray down on his desk.

Cornelius nodded.

"I am sure that he is fine, sir," the kindly kangaroo rat assured him.

"Perhaps . . ." Cornelius sighed. "But I simply must do something."

"If I might make a suggestion, sir," Mrs. Wiggins offered, "you could take your carriage out for a ride."

"I am in no mood for a ride," Cornelius said flatly.

"Even if the drive were in the direction of . . . a big city? Isn't that where Timothy always wanted to go? How about Varmintsville?"

"A sterling idea, Mrs. Wiggins!" Cornelius cried.

Minutes later Cornelius had hooked up his horse and was flying down the road to Varmintsville. As he rounded each bend and topped each hill, he kept his eyes peeled for Timothy. When he had to stop to rest, he was sure to ask the innkeeper to wake him at dawn.

Timothy was, of course, in Varmintsville. And he was getting hungrier with every hour. Just when he was about to give up hope, he noticed a sign in the window of a restaurant which read "Help Wanted." He was given a job there serving tables.

The restaurant was called "The Slop Shoppe," and Timothy soon discovered why. As the customers began arriving for breakfast, he noticed that they were not mice, rats, or rodents of any kind. They were pigs. His job was to carry large platters piled high with slop out to a dining room full of pigs, who would immediately begin shoving gobs of it into their chubby mouths.

"Good slop!" one of the pigs oinked. "But we're plenty hungry, so keep it comin'."

"Yeah, hurry it up, mouse!" another snorted.

"What a great mouse I have turned out to be," Timothy thought, as he scurried back to the kitchen. "Serving breakfast to a bunch of pigs. And I'm so hungry that even this slop is beginning to look good."

As Timothy continued to serve the hungry hogs, day after day, he made a decision.

"I would quite prefer my old life in the country to this," he confessed one morning. "I wonder if my father would take me back as an apprentice appletender. Even working in the cheeseworks, carting cheese wheels back and forth . . ."

"More slop over here!" a customer grunted.

"I do believe it's worth finding out," Timothy told himself.

So when the pigs were too busy gulping down slop to notice, Timothy apologized to the owner and left, snatching up his blue suitcase and scampering down the alleyway as fast as his legs would carry him.

It was just that day and just after noon when Timothy's father decided to stop for lunch. His horse had been galloping at top speed, and after reaching the crest of a hill, Cornelius directed his horse over to the side of the road.

He fed the horse, then nibbled on a cheddar cheese muffin and drank a tall glass of cool apple juice. As he stepped to the front to check if the horse had finished his oats, Cornelius spotted something down the road. He couldn't quite make out what it was, only that it was moving. After studying it for some time, he decided that it was an animal of some sort walking up the road.

"Could that be . . . ?" Cornelius wondered. And then he noticed something blue in the animal's paw.

"It is!" he shouted. "I know it is! Timothy, my son!" And he bolted down the hill to meet him.

Timothy had been walking for what seemed like days. His stomach was still growling, and his feet had already grown weary. Pausing at the side of the road to rest for a moment, he heard something. It sounded like someone yelling. Looking up the road he noticed an animal running toward him, flailing his arms and shouting something he couldn't quite make out.

Could it be? he wondered. And then he saw the old carriage parked on top of the hill.

"It is!" he shouted, dropping his suitcase. "Father! Oh, Father!" And he scurried up the hill to meet him.

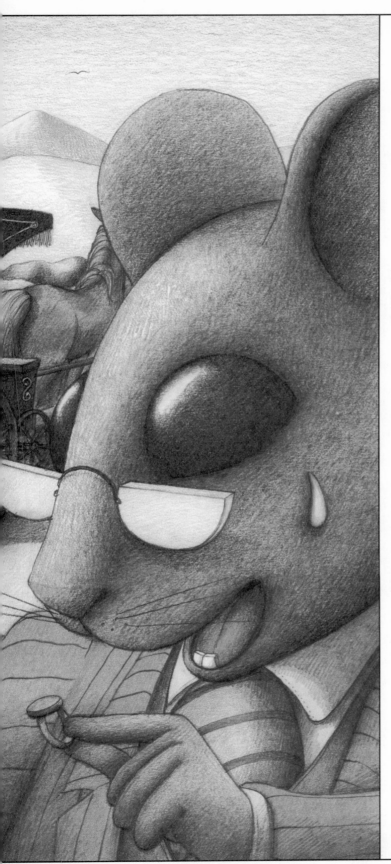

In a few moments the two mice were hugging each other tightly and exchanging kisses as tears streamed down both of their faces.

"Father, I'm so sorry," Timothy blubbered. "I was so foolish. I am not worthy to be your son. But please let me come back home. I'll do anything—dig tree holes, sort out rotten apples, even work in the cheeseworks . . . anything."

Cornelius grabbed Timothy by the shoulders.

"Not so fast," he said sternly, the smile disappearing from his face. "You left home, went to a faraway land, and squandered your inheritance, I suspect."

Timothy bowed his head in shame. "And . . . I don't have the ring you gave me."

"And now you come running back to me," Cornelius said, "expecting me to give you a job?"

"I just thought that . . . " Timothy stuttered.

"I won't hear of it," Cornelius scowled. "Any son of mine who returns home will be given nothing less—than a full partnership!" he said, the scowl turning into a smile as he patted Timothy on the back. "And about that ring," he said, pulling the gold band from his own finger, "here, take mine."

Cornelius and Timothy raced home in the carriage, stopping only at night, and made it back to the estate one afternoon just before supper. "Mrs. Wiggins! Mrs. Wiggins!" Cornelius shouted as they pulled up. "It's Timothy! Prepare one of your extra-special occasion suppers. Invite all our friends and neighbors! Timothy is back!" And he ordered a dapper new suit of clothes and a shiny new pair of shoes for Timothy.

Samuel, who had been hard at work in the cheeseworks all day, was just returning home when the celebration began. Hearing music, he looked in through the window, and saw animals eating and laughing. Then he saw Mrs. Wiggins coming out the back door to get something.

"What's all the fuss?" he asked with a puzzled look on his face.

"Oh, Samuel, it's so exciting!" the kindly kangaroo rat said. "Your brother Timothy has come home!"

"Oh, is that all?" he grumbled. "I figured he'd be back, sooner or later."

"Your father has ordered an extra-special supper, his best cheese and apples, all because Timothy has returned safe and sound," Mrs. Wiggins said. "Come join the party!"

"A fool's return is no reason to celebrate," Samuel said snootily. "I believe I'll just stay out here, thank you."

Mrs. Wiggins looked worried and hurried in to tell Cornelius that Samuel would not join the party.

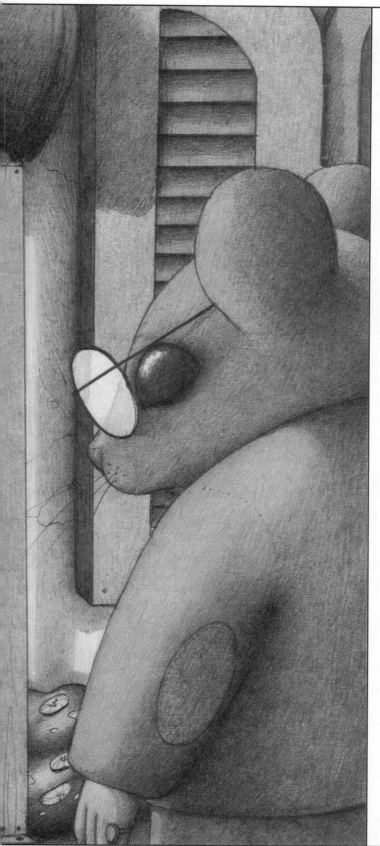

Cornelius came out right away. "Samuel, come greet your brother," Cornelius said with a smile.

"I will not," Samuel said stubbornly.

"But why?" he asked.

"All of these years I have worked for you, Father," Samuel complained, "laboring in the cheeseworks day and night. And you've *never* thrown me a party. Yet when foolish young Timothy leaves home and spends your money and then returns—"

"Samuel, my dear son," Cornelius grinned. "Don't you understand? I *know* that you are faithful and trustworthy. You are always with me and all that I have is yours. You know that. But your brother Timothy was as good as gone, lost in the big city, and now he has come back to us again. We certainly must celebrate."

Samuel frowned. He understood, but he didn't think it was fair.

"Come inside," Cornelius said. "Come greet your brother."

Samuel didn't want to at first, but he finally went inside and shook hands with Timothy.

The next day, after the party was over, Cornelius called Samuel and Timothy into his study.

"Now," he said with a smile, "let the three of us work together to make Cornelius T. Mouse & Sons a success, offering apples by the bushel and cheese by the wheel."

And in the following days, they did just that.

The End

You can read a story like this in the Bible. Jesus told it in Luke 15:11-32:

There was a man who had two sons. The younger one said to his father, "Father, give me my share of the estate." So he divided his property between them.

Not long after that, the younger son got together all he had, set off for a distant country, and there squandered his wealth in wild living. After he had spent everything, there was a severe famine in that whole country, and he began to be in need. So he went and hired himself out to a citizen of that country, who sent him to his fields to feed pigs. He longed to fill his stomach with the pods that the pigs were eating, but no one gave him anything.

When he came to his senses, he said, "How many of my father's hired men have food to spare, and here I am starving to death! I will set out and go back to my father and say to him: 'Father, I have sinned against heaven and against you. I am no longer worthy to be called your son; make me like one of your hired men.'" So he got up and went to his father.

But while he was still a long way off, his father saw him and was filled with compassion for him; he ran to his son, threw his arms around him, and kissed him.

The son said to him, "Father, I have sinned against heaven and against you. I am no longer worthy to be called your son."

But the father said to his servants. "Quick! Bring the best robe and put it on him. Put a ring on his finger and sandals on his feet. Bring the fattened calf and kill it. Let's have a feast and celebrate. For this son of mine was dead and is alive again; he was lost and is found." So they began to celebrate. . . .